To: Leif
Have fun and always swing for the fences!
Leslie Roberts

A Kid's LOOK at Big League Baseball

Written and Illustrated by Leslie Roberts

(with the help of Harper Roberts, age 8)

The contents of this work, including, but not limited to, the accuracy of events, people, and places depicted; opinions expressed; permission to use previously published materials included; and any advice given or actions advocated are solely the responsibility of the author, who assumes all liability for said work and indemnifies the publisher against any claims stemming from publication of the work.

All Rights Reserved
Copyright © 2023 by Leslie Roberts

No part of this book may be reproduced or transmitted, downloaded, distributed, reverse engineered, or stored in or introduced into any information storage and retrieval system, in any form or by any means, including photocopying and recording, whether electronic or mechanical, now known or hereinafter invented without permission in writing from the publisher.

Dorrance Publishing Co
585 Alpha Drive
Pittsburgh, PA 15238
Visit our website at *www.dorrancebookstore.com*

ISBN: 979-8-8852-7393-0
eISBN: 979-8-8852-7495-1

This book is tricky.

The pages on the right-hand side tell
the story of what happens when you go
to a big league baseball game.

The pages on the left-hand side show
photographs and tell interesting facts about
some big stadiums in different parts of America.

You can read all the pages on the right first
and then go back at look at the photographs;
or you can just bounce back and forth.

However you choose to read it, I hope this book
makes you want to go to a ball game. Have fun!

Camden Yards, where the Orioles play, fits right down in the city of Baltimore, Maryland. The architects even used a big old factory building as one wall of the stadium.

Do you play baseball? Do you just play in the yard or do you play on a team with uniforms? Someday you might play on a high school team or a college team.

If you are very, very good, you might become a Major League baseball player —and make a lot of money!

Major League teams play in big, fancy stadiums with thousands of cheering* fans in the stands.

Major League stadiums are usually in big cities.

*Or maybe they are booing...

Here is a ticket to a World Series game played in Atlanta, Georgia. The Atlanta Braves won the World Series in 2021.

Let's pretend you are going to a game. What will you see or hear or smell?

First, you will enter one of the main gates around the field. An usher will check your ticket. It could be a piece of paper in your hand—or a barcode on a cell phone. Right now, you should say "thank you" to the adult who brought you and maybe even give that person a hug because you can bet they paid big money for your ticket.

Yankee Stadium in New York City is a very famous ballpark in America. Doesn't it look cool at night?

When you go in the actual stadium to find your seat, your eyes may pop out! So much beautiful green grass, so many people, such a big scoreboard!

There will be music playing from loudspeakers, and there may be a video on the scoreboard.

Before you sit down, you will probably want to get some of that food you are smelling.

The Houston Astros sell fried chicken and mashed potatoes in an ice cream cone.

At T-Mobile Park in Seattle, you can buy fried grasshoppers—really!

Eating at the ballpark is a big part of the fun! You can buy a hot dog or a hamburger or chicken tenders or nachos with cheese or Crackerjacks or popcorn or ice cream or peanuts or cotton candy or almost anything you want! Let's hope you brought a big chunk of your allowance—or you came with someone like your grandma, who will spoil you.

The Philadelphia Phillies play in Philadelphia, Pennsylvania. But in this picture, they are the visiting team, lined up for the National Anthem before they play the San Francisco Giants in California.

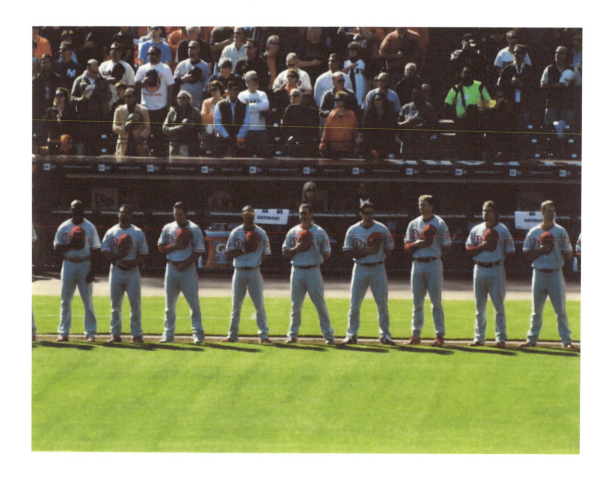

When you finally get to your seat, you are just in time! All the players are lined up on the baselines, and someone is singing "The National Anthem." The people in the stands will stand up and be very quiet unless they are singing along.*

When the song is over, all the people will shout PLAY BALL!!

The national anthem starts, "Oh, say, can you see…" Do you know the words?

Wrigley Field in Chicago, Illinois is one of the most famous stadiums in America. The Chicago Cubs have been playing baseball in this ballpark for more than 100 years!

Thanks to David Bearden for this special photo.

The home team (the game is in their park) will take the field first. The first batter for the visiting team will be up at home plate. Their next batter will be *on deck*.
This is how the field will look.

The people who build Major League ballparks want their stadiums to be different from others. Kauffman Stadium in Kansas City, Missouri, has a bank of fountains in the outfield that light up in different colors.

In the game, two main things will happen. The batter will try to hit the ball, and the pitcher will try to throw the ball so the batter <u>can't</u> hit it.

Pitchers can't just throw the ball anywhere. They have to throw it in the strike zone (between the batter's knees and shoulders). If the pitch misses the strike zone, it is a ball. If the pitcher throws four balls, the batter can just trot to first base for free.

Good pitchers can throw the ball really fast (close to 100 mph), but they also have tricky pitches, like curve balls, that can fool the batter and make him swing and miss.

Oracle Park in San Francisco, California, is built right on the bay. Fans come out in all kinds of boats, hoping to catch a home run ball hit out of the park.

The batter will be watching the pitches very carefully. If he swings at the ball and misses, the umpire* will call STRIKE ONE! If the batter gets three strikes, he is out, and his turn is over.

When the batter hits the ball, he starts running to first base. If any player on the other team catches the ball while it is in the air, the batter is out. If the ball goes all the way over the playing field in the air, it is a home run.

*Oops, I almost forgot. The umpires are those four people on the field wearing black shirts. One is standing behind home plate, and the others are near each base. They make the decisions about who is safe and who is out.

PNC Park in Pittsburgh, Pennsylvania, is the home of the Pittsburgh Pirates. It is built close to the Allegheny River, giving the fans a beautiful view of the river and downtown.

Usually, the batter is just happy to get a *hit*—that means he reached a base safely. The next batter may also get a hit, and the runners will *advance* to the next base. Any time a batter makes it around all the bases and steps on home plate, he scores a run for his team.

When the first team gets three outs, the teams will change places, and the home team will bat.

When each team has had their turn to bat, the inning is over. There are nine innings in a regular game.

Not all scoreboards look alike, but they all have this information.

									B	S	O
Inning	1	2	3	4	5	6	7	8	9	R	H	E
Visitor												
Home												

A few stadiums are covered with a roof that can be opened or closed. This is called a retractable roof. The roof over American Family Field in Milwaukee, Wisconsin, might keep out the snow in April or October.

Half of an inning can be long (the batters just keep getting on base and scoring) — or it can be very short (the pitcher strikes out 3 batters in a row).

After the visiting team has finished batting in the first half of the 7th inning, here comes the famous **7th Inning Stretch**! All the people watching the game will stand up, stretch their legs, and sing "Take Me Out to the Ball Game."

Then they will settle back down to watch the rest of the game—or maybe they will head for home if their team is losing.

Inning	1	2	3	4	5	6	7	8	9	R	H
Visitor	2	0	0	2	1	0	2			7	10
Home	1	0	1	2	3	0				6	9

I don't care if I never get back! 🎵

At Comerica Park in Detroit, Michigan, there are pictures, statues, and sculptures of tigers everywhere. A carousel inside the park has tigers to ride on. Can you guess the name of the team?

The Detroit Tigers!

Maybe you will get to stay until the end of the game, or maybe you will have to go home because it has gotten too late.

Either way, you will go home tired and happy because you have had a big fun time at a Major League baseball game!

Look on the next page for some more important stuff.

There is another level of professional baseball called the Minor Leagues. Minor League teams play in cities and towns all over America. These teams have clever and interesting names like:

Omaha Storm Chasers

Richmond Flying Squirrels

Albuquerque Isotopes

The players in the Minor Leagues want to develop their skills so that they will be called up to play on a Major League team. When that happens, they call it *going to the Show.*

Which team would you want to play for if you could *go to the Show?*

Printed in the USA
CPSIA information can be obtained
at www.ICGtesting.com
LVHW072231220324
775054LV00003B/5